CHILDREN'S SERMONS
for the Revised Common Lectionary
Year C

CHILDREN'S SERMONS
for the Revised Common Lectionary
Year C
Using the 5 Senses to Tell God's Story

PHILIP D. SCHROEDER

ABINGDON PRESS
Nashville

Children's Sermons for the Revised Common Lectionary
Year C
Copyright © 1997 by Abingdon Press

Scripture quotations, unless otherwise noted, are from the New Revised Standard Version Bible, Copyright © 1989, by the Division of Christian Education of the National Council of the Churches of Christ in the USA. Used by permission.

This book is printed on recycled, acid-free paper.

Book design by J. S. Lofbomm

Schroeder, Philip D., 1964-
    Children's sermons for the revised common lectionary : using the 5 senses to tell God's story / Philip D. Schroeder.
        p.   cm.
    Contents: [1].   Year A—[2].   Year B—[3].   Year C.
    ISBN 0-687-04996-2 (pbk.   :   v. 1   :   alk. paper). —ISBN 0-687-01827-7 (pbk.   :   v. 2   :   alk. paper). —ISBN 0-687-05577-6 (pbk.   :   v. 3   : alk. paper)
    1. Children's sermons.   2. Preaching to children.   3. Common lectionary (1992)   4. Lectionary preaching.   I. Title.
    BV4315.S335   1997
    251'. 53—dc21   97-14948
                                                                              CIP

97 98 99 00 01 02 03 04 05 06—10 9 8 7 6 5 4 3 2 1

MANUFACTURED IN THE UNITED STATES OF AMERICA

For our children
Daniel, Kathryn, and Paul

CONTENTS ——————————————

Foreword 9
First Sunday of Advent 29
Second Sunday of Advent 30
Third Sunday of Advent 31
Fourth Sunday of Advent 32
Christmas Eve/Christmas Day 33
First Sunday After Christmas Day 33
Epiphany of the Lord 34
Baptism of the Lord 35
Second Sunday After the Epiphany 36
Third Sunday After the Epiphany 37
Fourth Sunday After the Epiphany 38
Fifth Sunday After the Epiphany 39
Sixth Sunday After the Epiphany 40
Seventh Sunday After the Epiphany 41
Last Sunday After the Epiphany 42
First Sunday in Lent 43
Second Sunday in Lent 44
Third Sunday in Lent 45
Fourth Sunday in Lent 46
Fifth Sunday in Lent 47
Passion/Palm Sunday 48
Easter Day 49
Second Sunday of Easter 50
Third Sunday of Easter 51

Fourth Sunday of Easter 52
Fifth Sunday of Easter 52
Sixth Sunday of Easter 53
Ascension of the Lord/Seventh Sunday of Easter 54
Day of Pentecost 55
Trinity Sunday 56
Proper 4 57
Proper 5 58
Proper 6 59
Proper 7 60
Proper 8 62
Proper 9 63
Proper 10 64
Proper 11 65
Proper 12 66
Proper 13 67
Proper 14 68
Proper 15 68
Proper 16 69
Proper 17 70
Proper 18 71
Proper 19 72
Proper 20 73
Proper 21 74
Proper 22 75
Proper 23 76
Proper 24 77
Proper 25 78
Proper 26 79
Proper 27 80
Proper 28 81
Proper 29 83
Notes 84
Scripture Index 85

FOREWORD ————————

Extension agents in Georgia relate this story about the possibilities for children to act as catalysts for change. It seems that the newly appointed cooperative extension agent was struggling to convince the local farmers to use all the new and innovative farming methods being touted by the University of Georgia. He knew that such methods and ideas would increase the size and quality of vegetable production for these farmers. The agent went from farm to farm trying to convince any farmer who would listen of the advantages of his "newfangled" ways of planting and fertilizing, but the farmers wouldn't hear of it. They weren't going to have an outsider come into their county and tell them that their granddaddy's way of planting corn wasn't good enough anymore. Like that old-time religion, that old-time agriculture was good enough for them.

Then the extension agent came up with a brilliant idea. Why not hold a contest for the children of the community to see who could grow the best produce? A Corn Club was begun for boys as they tried to grow the biggest ears of corn. A Tomato Club was started for the girls who grew, harvested, and canned the most tomatoes from their family's gardens. The competition had implications beyond winners and losers. Increased corn production meant more money for the family and more grain to feed the farm animals. Canned tomatoes provided many meals for families who had to grow their own food. Miraculously, many of the children began to reap more bountiful harvests than their parents, the farmers. Through their children, the parents were indirectly invited into learning the new processes and were not threatened by the new ideas, for these were "just kids." Soon the adults began to ask how they, too, could grow such beautiful produce, and in stepped the same cooperative extension agent to share these "newfangled" methods with the eager farmers, who had been transformed by the seeds their children and the county extension agent had planted. What started in 1917 as Corn and Tomato Clubs are known as 4-H Clubs today.

Using children as the catalyst for change is not a new idea. Jesus himself pulled a child from the crowd to make a point in his own process for stimulating renewal. His methods featured parables that shattered preconceptions and left his listeners holding the paradox! Applying this concept of children acting as agents of change to the worship setting can provide an avenue for congregational transformation. Children hold promise and can lead the way through the sands shifting beneath our feet and into the new paradigms emerging in front of our eyes, ears, mouths, hands, and noses. Too often children are seen as agents of destruction because they seemingly disturb the solemnity of the sanctuary, but their very presence often sets a community of faith in motion.

Significant and meaningful change within the church can take place only if we recognize the importance of tradition. Items of value are not destroyed or replaced, but are disassembled, reorganized, and then rebuilt into a new creation by the God who makes all things new using the same building blocks. Children, the most recently created, can help us in the learning process of rebuilding for the future.

In a recent interview, Bill Gates, the mind behind Microsoft, commented that children are not necessarily more proficient than adults, but rather more willing to learn. He said that adults for the most part are unwilling to put up with the several hours of confusion necessary to learn basic computer skills. Children, on the other hand, are in a learning curve all the time and are often "confused" at the proliferation of data. They abide momentary darkness in hope of light better than adults.[1]

An Objection to the Object Lesson

Worship is a mystery, not a collection of skills to master or a body of knowledge to be understood. It is an experience to be lived. We learn to worship by worshiping! Children learn to worship by collecting experiences of worship.[2]

The majority of modern homiletical techniques focus on the two-dimensional illustration, the word picture, as the customary approach to the preaching task. The preacher seeks to illuminate a text with examples, stories, and analogies that help the listener hear and understand the message of the text in contemporary terms. To illustrate literally means to light up. Light allows the object to be examined more closely, but it remains an object. The *object lesson*, the most common method for sharing the gospel with children, asks children not only to make cognitive metaphorical connections that are beyond their grasp, but also to remain objective, never becoming subjects of the gospel.

TRY THIS EXPERIMENT: Assemble a group of children in a room. Place a painting on one side of the room; on the other side, place a television playing a children's video. Where will the children gravitate? Your experiment will probably show that the shift from the still life picture to the moving picture has already occurred in the lives of your children.

The children's sermon seems trapped in the age of the still life illustration or object lesson, the product of an earlier era. William Armstrong, author of the late-nineteenth-century book entitled *Five Minute Sermons to Children*, also struggled to find the most appropriate way to share the gospel with children. He understood that preaching to children took preparation but soon discovered that thirty minutes was too long for children's time! He finally settled on a five-minute children's sermon period that took into consideration his audience's attention span. His methodology is briefly summarized in the final words of his preface:

> Illustration is a necessity in all preaching (witness that of Christ), but especially in preaching to children. We all love pictures, but children love them most, and an illustration is a word-picture. An object sermon, if short and pointed, has a fine effect.[3]

Although Jesus did paint word pictures, it appears that he used far more than just object lessons to bring the gospel to life. Jesus was a multisensory teacher. He taught in ways that stimulated all the senses. Tasting, hearing, touching, seeing, and smelling were all part of his ministry.

Jesus helped those around him to taste and see that the Lord is good. He ate with sinners and tax collectors. He kept a party going by transforming water into wine. He taught the disciples by gathering grain to eat on the Sabbath. He broke bread and shared wine with his disciples who literally tasted the good news. Even after the Resurrection, Jesus asked for something to eat.

Jesus proclaimed the kingdom of God with his voice, and the people heard in new ways. He taught in parables that encouraged the hearers to listen, to reflect, and to respond. He invited people into the frames of his stories to struggle with the challenge of his words.

Jesus was constantly touching people while others struggled to touch him. When Jesus touched people to heal them, those around him claimed that in that touching, he taught with authority.

Jesus gave sight to people who had no sight and insight to the sighted. He pointed out scenes in their lives such as the widow's mite and told them to look at a coin to see whose picture was on it. He reminded them, "Blessed are the poor in spirit, for theirs is the kingdom of heaven."

Jesus was anointed for burial by Mary, Lazarus and Martha's sister. As the smell of that perfume drifted through the air, he taught of his impending death. (Jesus never seems to heal anyone who could not smell, but I suspect the lack of an olfactory capacity was a blessing in those days.)

Jesus used all the senses to communicate his message.

Swiss psychologist Jean Piaget argued that children actively construct reality out of their experiences with the environment rather than mimick what they encounter. Children live and learn rather than learn to live in the environment that is already in place. Everything does not have to be explained as it occurs, but as the child develops, she will begin to categorize and theologize about her experiences and draw her own conclusions.

In the first approximately two years of life, the sensorimotor period, children perceive only the existence of things that are within the immediate grasp of their senses. If they cannot taste, hear, touch, see, or smell something, it no longer exists in their world construct. This childhood stage features a sense of connectedness to all things. The child does not have a sense of where her body stops and everything else begins.[4]

This stage informs our human difficulty with affirming a God we cannot know through our senses. If an infant believes only in what she can sense, then are we not all infants in many ways? Children learn in this stage not by impersonal abstractions or arm's length study, but by an active physical interaction with the animate persons and inanimate objects in their lives. This stage is a time of exploring the world around them. Therefore, the children's sermon can be another opportunity for such exploration. It can be a safe time to learn to trust their environment and those around them. Children's sermons can respond to a child's search for things that are trustworthy in life. This first stage of learning, the lowest common denominator shared by all of humanity, can be the starting point for the children's sermon. If the children's sermon appeals to sensorimotor experiences, it will connect with all people on some level.

Object lessons may stimulate the senses of seeing, hearing, and touching, but there is little interaction with the object. At a church I recently visited, I listened as the minister showed the children a picture of an elephant. He asked the children, "How many of you have acted like elephants this week?" Blank stares were the response. A sensorimotor children's sermon on the same subject might have given each child the chance to behave like an elephant and discuss that behavior rather than merely talk about how elephants act. Object lessons allow people to remain objective, maintaining an "I-It" relationship; but Jesus set people in motion toward "I-Thou" relationships with God and one another. Jesus began a movement, yet many persons have sought to make him the object of their worship, an icon to be worshiped on the desktop of life. The life of Jesus is then used to illustrate a point instead of allowing his presence to be experienced in our daily lives. Christianity is not a still life picture, but a moving, spirited faith.

The Alternative—The Multisensory Subject Lesson

Multimedia can be defined as the confluence of written text, graphics such as photos, videos, illustrations, animation, and sound, such as speech and music to achieve a multisensory stimulation. Many multimedia computer programs have been labeled as "edutainment" products as the boundaries between learning and play have begun to blur. Computers allow for interactive learning when new lessons are constantly reinforced through the use of multiple senses at once.

Retention levels for all types of learning increase drastically when more than one sense is used to transmit the message.

> *TRY THIS EXERCISE: Make a list of all the scripture passages you have memorized. Now make a list of all the hymns you know by heart. Which list is longer?*

When words and melodies are combined, our minds retain more information. Multisensory children's sermons can help children to recall more of what has been presented, even though conveying factual knowledge is not the sole purpose of the children's sermon. Contrary to popular belief, entertainment for the children or the adults is not the goal of the children's sermon. Interestingly enough, entertainment has long been associated with passivity on the part of the one being entertained, but now entertainment is more participative than ever as people search for primary experiences. Children's sermons are more about experiencing the gospel for transformation and formation rather than for information or entertainment. Children learn by doing.

Children's sermons can be designed to develop relationships, establishing a level of trust between the leaders and the children while helping youngsters discover God in their own lives by hearing and participating in the retelling of the stories of God's people.

The same phenomenon seems to have found its way into many of our mainline Protestant churches as a congregation of spectators watch one person regulating the interaction. The sermon takes the form of a lecture, and the people are expected to consume the product being presented without response. In the silent print medium, there is no way of knowing whether or not you have, in fact, communicated your point when a person reads a document that you have written. Critiques and reviews of your presentation only continue the muted volleying between monologues. The shift in homiletics toward including an experience moves the people in the pews from observers to participants. By surrendering interpretive control of the presented experience, the sensorimotor children's sermon experience invites interaction between the worship leader, the children, and the entire congregation.

TRY ANOTHER EXPERIMENT: This time, instead of two choices, add a third dimension. Place a painting on one side of the room, a television with a VCR playing a video on another side of the room, and a multimedia computer displaying the most recently released Living Book CD-ROM in another spot. To which side will the children gravitate? A few children will still turn to the television to be entertained. Others will be fascinated with their ability to interact with the CD-ROM program, but only one child will ultimately be able to do so. Children sitting on the sidelines observing the multimedia presentation may soon opt for the television, since only one person can regulate the computer interaction.

If we trace the evolution of the video game, the shift in the perspective of the player in relationship to the game suggests this contemporary movement from observer to participant. The first video game, PONG, allowed the player to manipulate objects on a screen in order to prevent a small ball of light from moving off the edge of the screen. The ball never came toward the player, but remained an object that merely floated back and forth across the screen. As technology improved, games such as Space Invaders gave the player the visual and auditory feeling that aliens were getting closer to the bottom of the screen, which is where the player's hands reside, but still the "I-It" relationship remained. Then innovative games began to feature characters that looked out of the screen toward the player. Actions were performed with the movement of a simple joystick and the pressing of various buttons.

Currently, video games have changed their perspective so the player is not merely a manipulator of pieces disconnected to his or her physical space. The player becomes one of the characters in the story. Racing games no longer feature tiny cars that move around a circular track fully displayed in front of the driver. The driver is invited to sit behind the wheel and drive down a road that opens up directly in front of him or her. The player not only moves the car, but the car is designed so as to make the driver feel the bumps in the road by shaking the steering wheel upon impact. This change in perspective moves the player from the position of an interested observer to an actual subject within the game.

Virtual reality invites us to a place where we become a part of the movement, a place where we can discover things for ourselves. Virtual reality, the experience of perceiving and interacting through sensors and effectors with a computer-modeled environment, is essentially about world building. Virtual reality creates places where drug researchers can assemble virtual molecules, where doctors can practice surgical skills on computer-generated patients, where astronauts can simulate Mars landings, and where architects can walk through dream homes. While many of these applications seem futuristic, virtual reality is already routinely used in airline flight simulators enabling pilots to hone their abilities to handle increasingly complex modern aircraft. Virtual reality provides a place for us to explore, to gain knowledge, and to practice skills we have acquired. With the advent of the multisensory experiences of multimedia and virtual reality, the dominant method of communication has shifted from the silently read, written word to the echoing and reverberating moving word.

During a recent visit to a virtual reality playground featuring an interactive exploration adventure, I found the most interesting aspect of the experience was not the game itself, but the manner in which potential players were taught the game. Recruits were herded into a room with a huge video screen where they watched an eight-minute movie. The movie portrayed other rookies participating in a real-life mission similar to our virtual one. Guidance was given only through this video parable of what happened to others in similar circumstances. The recruits were invited to become part of a continuing story by stepping into this virtual world.

Virtual reality in its current state has some severe limitations for use in the communication of the biblical text. As our earlier experiment illustrates, virtual reality often lacks a communal aspect and approaches the same individualism associated with the silently read text. I propose that the church embrace a *vital ritual reality* that takes the participatory stance of virtual reality and includes the virtues of the communal experience. As the community of faith gathers to share in the Eucharist, where the inanimate becomes animate, the story of our faith is not only retold, but also relived.

Vital ritual reality gives us the opportunity to relive the story with all our senses as we taste the wine, smell the bread, touch the hands of others, hear the words of forgiveness and consecration, and see the lifted cup and broken bread.

Our children and our churches need a *vital ritual reality* in which we can feel the power of the story of Christ with all our senses and thus celebrate a dynamic faith together.

Discovering and Designing Multisensory Interactive Children's Sermons

In the new system, the audio and the visual materials are not aids; they blend with the subject matter itself to evoke an experience.[5]

Take a deep breath and read the following passage aloud from beginning to end without stopping to catch your breath:

> For this reason I bow my knees before the Father, from whom every family in heaven and on earth takes its name. I pray that, according to the riches of his glory, he may grant that you may be strengthened in your inner being with power through his Spirit, and that Christ may dwell in your hearts through faith, as you are being rooted and grounded in love. I pray that you may have the power to comprehend, with all the saints, what is the breadth and length and height and depth, and to know the love of Christ that surpasses knowledge, so that you may be filled with all the fullness of God. Now to him who by the power at work within us is able to accomplish abundantly far more than all we can ask or imagine, to him be glory in the church and in Christ Jesus to all generations, forever and ever. Amen. (Eph. 3:14-21)

Reading this passage without pause communicates the connectedness of the text indirectly. Rather than declaring that, in their original form, these words of the Pauline Epistle were originally written as one long sentence, you, the reader, were asked to participate in one method of experiencing a text. This method transports the words off the written page into your mouth and into your mind. Multimedia presentations advertise the possibilities for a movement from the reading of a dry text to the reception of "an earful, an eyeful, and a mind full" of the ideas being communicated by the text. By your reading aloud, your relationship with the text has changed from observer of the silent print medium to participant in the continued life of the text.

Stage One: A Preparatory Posture

A close friend, Ginger Reedy, was attempting to make her home safe for her second child who was learning to walk. With her first child, Ginger had walked around the house picking up things and moving them to the next higher level so they wouldn't be dangerous for their older child, Sarah Linn, as she took her first steps. Unfortunately, Sarah Linn found innumerable items to explore and explode, in spite of her mother's best efforts. With this information from her history, Ginger took a new posture in preparing for her second child's adventure into walking. She got down on her knees, not to pray for the strength to deal with the child, but to inspect the house from a child's point of view. Ginger discovered that there were many things to be moved that she would never have thought of from her previous angle of vision.

The starting point for the preparation of the children's sermon is also a new posture, a preparatory posture. You might begin by performing a child's view accessibility audit of your sanctuary. Walk around the sanctuary on your knees to see what you discover from a child's perspective. I have yet to see a church with a children's pew where children can sit with their feet touching the floor. (Chairs from the children's Sunday school class would provide a temporary solution in some settings.)

Children are quite literally overlooked in many sanctuaries, and we do very little to dispel the notion that this is an "adults only" space. God chose to become like us physically in order to communicate God's love to us and save us. I propose this same physical incarnational approach to our sermons with children. Unless you turn and become like a child, not only will you miss the kingdom of God, but it will also be impossible for you to really connect with children.

Preparation for children's sermons is active, not merely intellectual. Children are noisy, messy, full of energy, and occasionally disruptive. Children enjoy moving, playing, and celebrating! They tumble in the grass, run down hills at full speed, do somersaults, and spin around in circles for no other reason than the physical activity and the release of energy.

Remembering the feeling of walking along a railroad track or a curb is not the same as going out and taking that walk again. We miss certain nuances if we rely solely on our memories of our childhood rather than take the time to participate in a childhood activity. Taking a preparatory posture brings us physically into a child's world. The preparatory posture re-members us into the community of children and helps us practice for the experiences to be shared with children in worship. Just as virtual reality provides practice for real-life situations, a *vital ritual reality* invites children and adults to practice their faith. Practice helps us move easily into actual situations and gives us tools to predict when something might go wrong. Practice is itself an experience that prepares us for other experiences. We practice our sermons for the adults—at least we are supposed to—but we don't seem to practice for our time with the children even when we do take the time to prepare.

We have applied the preparatory posture to the overall creation of children's sermons, but the children's sermon most often begins with the text. The Gospel lesson from the First Sunday of Advent of Year B of the Revised Common Lectionary is Mark 13:24-37.

What type of physical posture or movement emerges from this text?

But in those days, after that suffering,
  the sun will be darkened,
    and the moon will not give its light,
  and the stars will be falling from heaven,
    and the powers in the heavens will be shaken.

Then they will see 'the Son of Man coming in clouds' with great power and glory. Then he will send out the angels, and gather his elect from the four winds, from the ends of the earth to the ends of heaven.

From the fig tree learn its lesson: as soon as its branch becomes tender and puts forth its leaves, you know that summer is near. So also, when you see these things taking place, you know that he is near, at the very gates. Truly I tell you, this generation will not pass away until all these things have taken place. Heaven and earth will pass away, but my words will not pass away.

But about that day or hour no one knows, neither the angels in heaven, nor the Son, but only the Father. Beware, keep alert; for you do not know when the time will come. It is like a man going on a journey, when he leaves home and puts his slaves in charge, each with his work, and commands the doorkeeper to be on the watch. Therefore, keep awake—for you do not know when the master of the house will come, in the evening, or at midnight, or at cockcrow, or at dawn, or else he may find you asleep when he comes suddenly. And what I say to you I say to all: Keep awake. (Mark 13:24-37)

Possible Postures:
- Alertness, like a baseball player who keeps on his toes waiting for a ground ball or a child waiting for a parent to come home
- Asleep, curled up for a long nap
- Traveling, going on a trip, or a hike
- Yawning

The task of the preparatory posture is to encourage the sermon preparer to engage the text not only intellectually but also physically. The preparatory posture is a playful exercise. Too often we ask the children to think about waiting for Christmas or to recall trying to stay awake on Christmas Eve instead of actually creating the tension of waiting with the children as they gather. After a posture is identified, the leader is encouraged to take that stance during his or her time of preparation. Assuming a preparatory posture may mean taking a short hike, yawning a big yawn, or standing on your tiptoes. Doing this will probably feel silly at first, but it can be a valuable exercise. We communicate with children not only through our words, but also through body positions and body language. Children sense when we are uncomfortable with their postures. The preparatory posture becomes a plank from which to jump back into the text and begin the second stage of discovery.

Stage Two: The Experience

The question asked when designing the object lesson message is, "What object can I use to help me communicate a point based on the text to the children?" This method often falls prey to the "grab and stab" method of preparation as the worship leader searches the church in the minutes prior to the worship service trying to find a suitable object about which to make a point. Unfortunately, children will seldom retain the point that is trying to be forced upon them and will draw instead their own conclusions about the object in question.

If the intent of worship is to praise and experience God, the second stage poses the question, "How can I create an occasion during which the children can experience the story of God as set forth in the text?" We cannot give or teach faith to our children; we can only share the faith story as it has become our story and encourage the gift that is faith. The faith story is passed on by sharing, experiencing, and living the story together. Children and adults will grow in faith through shared experience and shared reflection.

While I was serving as an associate pastor to a church in Georgia, the senior minister was preparing to preach on "the pearl of great price." He asked me to compose a children's sermon from Matthew 13:45-46. It was not a lot to go on, but I tried to find a way for the children to engage in a search for a pearl of great value. Since pearls are usually found in oysters, I went to the local grocery store and bought a dozen oysters still in the shell. I rigged them so they were easy to open, and I forced a small pearl into one of the oysters. When the children came to the front of the church for children's time, we opened oysters together, looking for pearls. Finally, we opened one with a pearl, and the children were so excited that our search had been successful; we had found our own pearl of great value. They were not asked to recall feelings of searching and finding from their memories or told about my encounters with searching and finding. The children experienced the thrill of searching and joy of finding, which Jesus emphasized in Luke 15. These feelings can also be evoked by good storytelling and drama; but unlike what happens in storytelling, the children become a physical part of this story, and unlike what happens in drama, the children are themselves rather than the characters they portray.

I recall that particular children's sermon not for the idea I used, but for the feedback I received afterward. A father of two of the children at the children's sermon relayed to me the conversation that occurred on the drive home from the service. He and his wife were discussing the points of the senior minister's sermon when a voice from the backseat vaulted over into the fray. Their daughter recalled her experience with the search and added a new dimension to the family's faith journey. The children's sermon has a much greater value when seen as an integrated part of the entire service rather than when used as a break in the action to address the kids before they can be sent elsewhere.

The ritual dimension of our worship service is our faith community's theology in action. Ritual moves faith from the mind to the body as our ideas about God not only are thought out, but also become reality. A trip to the local science museum finds children running and jumping while learning about science. Discovering gravity and finding out about surface tension are not dull chores, but exciting experiences as the children are encouraged to drop things from various heights and make bubbles of all sizes. The cognitive development abilities of children are considered as this type of science education provides a playground for the senses. Learning about God can be just as exciting and experiential. We must begin to address children on their level instead of keeping them in the pew queue waiting for the time when they, too, can sit back and consume rather than produce worship. Liturgy has become the work of the clergy. Children, however, are not afraid to carry their part of the liturgical load.

Adults often see fastening their seat belts as a chore. My children see it as a game to test who can be buckled up the fastest. Now, it is not a case of whether or not to buckle my seat belt, but of how I can play this safety game with my kids. They have invited and encouraged me to do something that I may have failed to do myself. Children can play the same deconstructionist role for us in worship as they invite all of us into new experiences of God by their playfulness, informality, honesty, and willingness to explore.

When people recall meaningful worship services, they seldom use the language "I heard" or "I saw" the presence of God; rather, the sense of God is felt, experienced. We know God by participating in the text. Looking back to the first Gospel text in Advent, Year B, we ask the question, "How can we make this text accessible to children through their senses?" To find a multisensory experience, it helps to read the text with all the senses in mind. "Senses help us to think and react emotionally."[6] We taste the gospel at Communion, touch the gospel during baptism, and smell the gospel through the burning of incense.

Read Mark 13:24-37 again and make a list of what you sense from the text and what someone who was standing there listening to Jesus might have sensed.

- Sights: Clouds, falling stars, the gates, angels in heaven, Father, Son, Son of Man, darkness, doorkeeper watching for the Master
- Sounds: Cockcrow, keep awake, alarm, a ticking clock
- Tastes: Figs
- Smells: Fig trees, storm, winds
- Touches: Shaking, winds, gathering people, texture of fig leaves
- Feelings: Fear, waiting

Since we are forced to begin with a print medium, the Scriptures, sight and hearing are the givens for any sermon or children's sermon. The key is to layer as many senses within the children's sermon as possible, using taste, smell, and touch whenever possible. Even multimedia and virtual reality have not adequately included these senses in ways of which we are capable in the worship setting.

If we retain less than 15 percent of what we hear, oral sermons are like homiletical billboards posted all along the highway, seldom remembered or responded to beyond an immediate reaction. The task in creating a children's sermon is to discover what the children can do to experience the text rather than what they can be told about the text. Word pictures are no longer our primary means of communication.

When asked what they learned in school that day, young children primarily recount what they did, not what they learned. Children are doers! Their perceptions of what they do know are often distorted as one child in my first church recalled, "Mama, I do know my ABC's. It's just that my ABC's are different from your ABC's." Children learn the alphabet song and assume they know the alphabet. My children thought LMNO was a word, not a series of letters. Just because children can tell you they have learned something doesn't mean they can use it or apply it.

The intent of the children's sermon is to get children, as well as adults, thinking in new ways. Give children the text in a way they can understand. Allow them to discover the text and find meaning from the experience itself. Be willing to struggle with the loss of control as you are no longer making a point for the children or making points with the parents, but joining the children on a journey into the text and into faith.

Outline of the Methodology for Experiencing the Gospel

I. Select the Scripture text to be shared with the children.

A. Exegete the text. Decide if the children can connect in some way to the text. Note: not all texts are accessible to children.

B. If at all possible, use the same text to be used with the adults.

II. Identify preparatory postures within the text.

A. Assume at least one of the postures you have identified.

B. Move into the text physically in order to prepare for interaction with the children.

C. Have fun; remember this is a playful posture.

III. Search for sensory stimuli in the text.

A. List the stimuli as found in the five sensory categories:

1. Sight
2. Sound
3. Taste
4. Smell
5. Touch

B. Identify the senses that can be re-created in the worship setting.

C. Identify which of these senses will connect the experiences of children to the text.

1. Observe children in their interactions; listen to their language; taste the current fad food popular with children.
2. Use all of your senses to prepare.

IV. **Bring the text to life with a multisensory experience.**

    A. Attempt to use three or more senses.
    B. Allow the children to participate rather than observe.
    C. Ask open-ended questions to help the children reflect on their experience.

V. **Link the children's sermon to the adult's sermon and the entire worship service.**

    A. Use the same Scripture text (if possible).
    B. Invite the adults into an experience.
    C. Discuss with the entire congregation any questions that emerged from the children's sermon.

FIRST SUNDAY OF ADVENT
LECTIONARY READINGS
Jeremiah 33:14-16
Psalm 25:1-10
1 Thessalonians 3:9-13
Luke 21:25-36

TEXT: Luke 21:25-36

PREPARATORY POSTURE: Stand up. Raise your head and look at the clouds. Pray that you might have strength for the days to come.

EXPERIENCE: Prepare an Advent pep talk for the children complete with exercises to get them psyched for the days ahead. Luke's apocalyptic language at the end of Jesus' public ministry attempts to encourage the people in the same manner. "Stand up, raise your head, be on guard, and be alert" can be among the commands used with the children.

When a ball is flying through the air and about to hit someone, unless I am on a golf course, I yell, "Heads up!" What do most other people do? They cover their heads and look down. Try it with the kids and see what happens. With your head down, you can't catch the ball or even know how to avoid it; you can only be hit by the ball. When Jesus says, "Heads up!" he means heads UP. That's the only way we can catch the redemption Jesus is throwing to us. In verse 28, Jesus tells us that when others are covering their heads, scared of all the things around them, we should stand up and raise our heads so we can catch the good things God is sending us! Finish with a mantra such as

"Stand up," "Heads up," "Be alert" as the children begin their journey through Advent.

SENSES: *Hearing, sight, and touch*

SECOND SUNDAY OF ADVENT
LECTIONARY READINGS:
Malachi 3:1-4
Luke 1:68-79
Philippians 1:3-11
Luke 3:1-6

TEXT: Malachi 3:1-4

PREPARATORY POSTURE: Clean a piece of tarnished silver.

EXPERIENCE: Malachi is announcing the coming of the Lord's messenger who will change things for the better, but change is not always easy. Making things better can often be painful, as children know from shots, medicine that doesn't taste good, certain antiseptics on open cuts, or even brushing knotted hair. Ask the children about the things in their lives that hurt but could make them better in the long run. Finally, suggest getting scrubbed clean with soap and water, like fullers' soap, after a romp in the dirt.

Show the children a piece of tarnished silver. Talk about how years of handling and exposure to air makes the silver change colors. We can let things get dirtier and dirtier, but they look much nicer when we finally clean them up. Allow one of the children to dip the silver in a tarnish-removing solution. Pull the silver out, showing the miraculous change in color as a refiner of silver would have done. (The outer layer of the silver is actually removed.)

Discuss with the children the things that God would want to clean up in our lives and our communities.

SENSES: *Hearing, touch, and sight*

THIRD SUNDAY OF ADVENT
LECTIONARY READINGS:
Zephaniah 3:14-20
Isaiah 12:2-6
Philippians 4:4-7
Luke 3:7-18

TEXT: Luke 3:7-18

PREPARATORY POSTURE: Examine your closet for an extra coat that can be shared with someone in need.

EXPERIENCE: Use a musical scale or a series of words to create the feeling of expectation. Singing a scale from do to ti, do-re-mi-fa-sol-la-ti, begs for resolution and gives the distinct feeling that something comes next. Words and phrases, such as "Tomorrow we're going to . . . " or "All of a sudden . . .," can also provide pangs of anticipation. Talk about Advent as a time of expectation. The waiting crowds asked John, "What then should we do?"

Give the children this question to ask as you describe several situations such as a woman who had two winter coats. "What then should we do?" Give the extra coat to someone who has none. If you have two coats in your closet, bring one to leave on the altar. This might be the beginning of a winter coat collection for those who have none. Tell another story about a family with too much food: "What then should we do?" Share with someone who is hungry. Place some food from your own pantry on the altar

31

and begin an Advent food drive. The possibilities are endless. Encourage the children to go home and attempt to answer the question "What then should we do?" with their families. Allow the children to report how they answered their questions next Sunday or on Christmas Eve if time allows.

SENSES: *Hearing, touch, and sight*

FOURTH SUNDAY OF ADVENT
LECTIONARY READINGS:
Micah 5:2-5*a*
Luke 1:47-55
Hebrews 10:5-10
Luke 1:39-45 (46-55)

TEXT: Micah 5:2-5*a*

PREPARATORY POSTURE: Visit a farm and help feed the livestock.

EXPERIENCE: Send an older child or adult "shepherd" out of earshot and then discuss with the children what sheep are like. Be sure to tell them that sheep don't play Follow the Leader. They prefer to stay and eat right where they are. Sheep must be driven and not led. Then bring the would-be shepherd back and assign him or her the task of leading the sheep/children from one place to another in the sanctuary. Eventually, the shepherd will change from leading the sheep to driving the sheep as the children don't respond. Jesus is not out in front yelling for us to catch up; he is next to or behind us helping us along.

SENSES: *Hearing, sight, and touch*

CHRISTMAS EVE/CHRISTMAS DAY
LECTIONARY READINGS:
Isaiah 9:2-7/Isaiah 52:7-10
Psalm 96/Psalm 98
Titus 2:11-14/Hebrews 1:1-4 (5-12)
Luke 2:1-14 (15-20)/John 1:1-14

TEXTS: Luke 2:1-14 (15-20), Isaiah 9:2-7

PREPARATORY POSTURE: Make a list of all the names by which you refer to God/Jesus. Listen to Handel's *Messiah*.

EXPERIENCE: In the darkness of Christmas Eve, make the sanctuary as dark as possible, then shine a great light and read Isaiah 9:6-7 to the children. Dim the light and begin reading Luke 2:1-20. At verse 9, shine the light again as the angel speaks. Let the choir sing the part of the heavenly hosts in verse 14. Then lead the children to a manger scene where they can see the baby Jesus with Mary and Joseph. Send them back to their seats glorifying and praising God for what they have seen and heard.

SENSES: *Hearing, sight, and touch*

FIRST SUNDAY AFTER CHRISTMAS DAY
LECTIONARY READINGS:
1 Samuel 2:18-20, 26
Psalm 148
Colossians 3:12-17
Luke 2:41-52

TEXT: Luke 2:41-52

PREPARATORY POSTURE: Help a twelve-year-old boy or girl prepare to read the Gospel lesson this Sunday.

EXPERIENCE: Children will remember the child who was left behind by his parents in the movie *Home Alone*. They can probably recall many of the antics in which he participated. As a child, I always wondered why Jesus' parents would have left the city without him. One plausible explanation is that the men traveled in one group and the women traveled in another. Jesus was at the age where his father might have thought he was with the women and children, while his mother might have thought he was with the men. This knowledge calmed my fears about why Jesus was left behind. Other children might benefit from this knowledge.

Retell the story by splitting the children into groups of boys and girls. Pick a girl to be Mary and a boy to be Joseph. Send the girls down the aisle on their journey home. When the girls get halfway, send the boys. Be sure to tell the children that it was not because the girls were slower, but that they often carried the provisions and watched the children as they walked. When they arrive at the back of the church, help Mary and Joseph realize that Jesus is not with them. "I thought he was with you" is a line many of us parents have uttered. Send them back to the front where they will find a twelve-year-old boy reading his Bible. Have a dialogue between Jesus and his parents and/or let a twelve-year-old read the Gospel lesson for the congregation.

SENSES: *Hearing, touch, and sight*

EPIPHANY OF THE LORD
LECTIONARY READINGS:
Isaiah 60:1-6
Psalm 72:1-7, 10-14

Ephesians 3:1-12
Matthew 2:1-12

TEXT: Matthew 2:1-12

PREPARATORY POSTURE: Play a game of Hide and Go Seek Jesus with preschool children.

EXPERIENCE: If you have a manger scene displayed in the sanctuary, hide the baby Jesus before the service, and allow the children to search diligently for the child. You might even have a star placed on the ceiling above the place where the baby is hidden or a Herod who asks the children to tell him where the baby was born. Instruct the children to bring the baby Jesus back to the manger scene by a route that does not pass by Herod.

Ask the children if they would have told Herod where to find the baby Jesus. If possible, give each child a star and a baby Jesus to take home on this day of giving gifts. Encourage them to play the game with their families, for we are all searching for Jesus.

SENSES: *Hearing, sight, and touch*

BAPTISM OF THE LORD (First Sunday After the Epiphany)
LECTIONARY READINGS:
Isaiah 43:1-7
Psalm 29
Acts 8:14-17
Luke 3:15-17, 21-22

TEXT: Luke 3:15-17, 21-22

PREPARATORY POSTURE: Practice using a squirt gun.

EXPERIENCE: Use a concealed squirt gun or spray bottle to lightly put water on someone until the person turns away from you. John offered a water baptism of repentance for the forgiveness of sins. Repentance is a turning away from sin. Receiving the water of baptism was a symbol that the people were turning back toward God as they confessed their sins. Repeat John's words in Luke 3:16-17 for the children. Allow time for them to sink in as the children ponder their meaning. Answer any questions they might have. An actual winnowing fork and some grain might make answering their questions easier.

Emphasize that all were baptized, even Jesus. Continue the story, telling them that when Jesus was baptized and was praying, the heavens opened and the Holy Spirit descended upon him in bodily form like a dove. Then a voice came from heaven: "You are my Son, the Beloved; with you I am well pleased." If *well pleased* means "happy with," ask the children if God is well pleased with them.

Consider sending each child home with a bar of Dove soap so that parents and children can keep the symbols of water and the dove together while reminding them of the cleansing power of baptism as we all continue our journey toward an understanding of the mystery of the Holy Spirit.

SENSES: *Hearing, sight, smell, and touch*

SECOND SUNDAY AFTER THE EPIPHANY
LECTIONARY READINGS:
Isaiah 62:1-5
Psalm 36:5-10
1 Corinthians 12:1-11
John 2:1-11

TEXT: John 2:1-11

PREPARATORY POSTURE: Attend or observe a wedding reception.

EXPERIENCE: Prepare two pitchers—a clear pitcher and another made of pottery or any nontransparent material. Line the bottom of the second pitcher with purple-colored presweetened powder or liquid drink mix, or tape tea bags that produce reddish tea to the side of the container. Fill the clear pitcher with water, warm water if you use the tea bag option. (I have found that the tea bags and warm water are the most effective option, since as the water is poured back into the clear pitcher it looks clear at first, but then turns a deeper red as more and more liquid is poured out. Using tea bags also allows you to turn the second pitcher over before the clear water is poured into it to give the impression that the pitcher is empty.)

Introduce the story of Jesus' turning water into wine as the first sign that Jesus performed. Pour the water from the clear pitcher into the pitcher with the hidden drink. (Be sure to practice so you get a good mixture!) Then pour the water back into the clear pitcher for an amateurish turning of water into wine. Let the children taste the new mixture, just as the steward tasted the wedding wine. Stress the amazement of the people who witnessed the miracle and how Jesus kept the party going and going and going.

SENSES: *Hearing, sight, smell, taste, and touch*

THIRD SUNDAY AFTER THE EPIPHANY
LECTIONARY READINGS:
Nehemiah 8:1-3, 5-6, 8-10
Psalm 19

1 Corinthians 12:12-31a
Luke 4:14-21

TEXT: Luke 4:14-21

PREPARATORY POSTURE: Visit a synagogue. If possible, examine a scroll written in Hebrew.

EXPERIENCE: Tell the story of Jesus' arriving in his hometown synagogue on the Sabbath day. He stood up to read and was handed a scroll with words from the prophet Isaiah. Prepare a scroll for the children to read, but print the words from right to left as the Hebrew would be read rather than from left to right. Let a child unroll it. Help the child interpret the letters by showing him or her that it is not gibberish when read from right to left—for example, EM NOPU SI DROL EHT FO TIRIPS EHT for The Spirit of the Lord Is Upon Me. Give all the children a chance to read or unroll the scroll.

SENSES: *Hearing, sight, and touch*

FOURTH SUNDAY AFTER THE EPIPHANY
LECTIONARY READINGS:
Jeremiah 1:4-10
Psalm 71:1-6
1 Corinthians 13:1-13
Luke 4:21-30

TEXT: Jeremiah 1:4-10

PREPARATORY POSTURE: Visit someone who is about to or has just had a baby, and share the good news from Jeremiah.

EXPERIENCE: The children can relate to Jeremiah in this passage as he says, "I am only a boy." "But I'm just a kid! What can I do?" God touches Jeremiah's lips and states, "Now I have put my words in your mouth." A ventriloquist would be perfect for this text as the children see the thrown voice is literally words being put into the dummy's mouth. Let them see how the dummy works and ask them if they want to be "dummies for God," or "fools for the sake of Christ," in Paul's words.

Touch each child's mouth and repeat Jeremiah 1:9b, "Now I have put my words in your mouth." Assure them that God can use all people, no matter how old or young they might be. Show them examples from the congregation of people of all ages whom God has called to ministry. Close with the reassuring words in Jeremiah 1:5,

> Before I formed you in the womb I knew you,
> and before you were born I consecrated you;
> I appointed you a prophet to the nations.

SENSES: *Hearing, sight, taste, and touch*

FIFTH SUNDAY AFTER THE EPIPHANY
LECTIONARY READINGS:
Isaiah 6:1-8 (9-13)
Psalm 138
1 Corinthians 15:1-11
Luke 5:1-11

TEXT: Luke 5:1-11

PREPARATORY POSTURE: Walk along the side of a lake. Feed the fish.

EXPERIENCE: Children have played a variety of tag games from Freeze Tag to Tunnel Tag. Teach them a new game called Fish Tag. Simon Peter, James, and John were fishermen. Tell the children the story of the net-breaking catch and Peter's confession. Discuss what it means to make a confession. It is the first step to getting things right with other people and with God, confessing that we have done something wrong. Peter must think he is going to be punished, and he is afraid, just as children are when they expect punishment. Instead of offering punishment, Jesus tells Peter not to be afraid and that he will be catching people from then on.

Fish Tag is simple. Tag one of the children and say, "You're God's," instead of "You're It." Instruct the child to respond to the tag by standing up. Then the two of you can tag two other people and say, "You're God's." Send the children out to tag the whole congregation. Make sure everyone is tagged. Close by sending everyone out to catch people for Christ, not to catch them doing bad things as Peter thought, but to catch them with the net of God's love.

SENSES: *Hearing, sight, and touch*

SIXTH SUNDAY AFTER THE EPIPHANY
LECTIONARY READINGS:
Jeremiah 17:5-10
Psalm 1
1 Corinthians 15:12-20
Luke 6:17-26

TEXT: Luke 6:17-26

PREPARATORY POSTURE: Jump as high as you can.

EXPERIENCE: Gather the children and have them stand on one level in the sanctuary. Have the children remain standing as you sit down. Verse 20 tells us that Jesus looked up at his disciples and began to repeat the blessings: "Blessed are you who are poor. . . . Blessed are you who are hungry now. . . ." Talk to the children about the meaning of these blessings. Do they fit into any of the categories? Do they know someone who does? Tell them a story of a Christian martyr who suffered for his or her belief in Christ.

Hold up a sign well out of the children's reach with the word *Joy* printed on it. Let them take turns leaping for joy. When everyone has had a chance, bring the sign down to their level and let everyone touch it, or give everyone a copy because joy comes to us when we do what God wants us to do.

SENSES: *Hearing, sight, and touch*

SEVENTH SUNDAY AFTER THE EPIPHANY
LECTIONARY READINGS:
Genesis 45:3-11, 15
Psalm 37:1-11, 39-40
1 Corinthians 15:35-38, 42-50
Luke 6:27-38

Text: Luke 6:27-38

PREPARATORY POSTURE: Do something good for someone who dislikes you. Say a prayer of blessing for those who curse you. Pray for those who abuse you.

EXPERIENCE: With this text, I usually recount for the children a personal childhood encounter with a bully, which is easy for most of us, unless you were the bully. My father always taught me not to fight but to turn the other cheek. After numerous fights, I decided to try it. The bully hit me, and I offered my face up for the next blow. He got mad but couldn't hit me again. He finally walked away. It was the only time it ever worked. Yet I wonder how I could have gone the next step and made that enemy my friend.

Let the children talk about their enemies, and suggest ways to make them into friends. Be prepared to help the children deal with the bullies in their lives.

SENSES: *Hearing and sight*

LAST SUNDAY AFTER THE EPIPHANY
(Transfiguration Sunday)
LECTIONARY READINGS:
Exodus 34:29-35
Psalm 99
2 Corinthians 3:12–4:2
Luke 9:28-36 (37-43)

TEXTS: Luke 9:28-36 (37-43); 2 Kings 2:1-12

PREPARATORY POSTURE: Make a list of sins for which you want to repent. Pray a prayer of confession and burn the list.

EXPERIENCE: On this day of transfiguration, the appearance of Jesus' face changes. Offer to change the appearance of the children's faces with a cross of ashes. If you do not currently have a service of the Imposition of Ashes on Ash Wednesday, this children's sermon could introduce the service to the church through the children. Watching the children experience this ritual may deconstruct or lessen any adult resistance to what may be a new ritual for them and thus release new energy into your church. I have success-fully introduced the Imposition of Ashes to two rural churches by inviting the children to act as catalysts for deconstructing the established order.

The ashes can be gathered from the burning of last year's palm branches or from the burning of slips of paper on which the children have written things for which they want to be forgiven. Use the ashes to place a cross of ashes on the forehead of each child, saying, "Remember that you are dust and to dust you shall return." You might also want to include some of the older children in the preparation of the ashes. God's presence with us can change the way we appear to others.

SENSES: *Hearing, sight, smell, and touch*

FIRST SUNDAY IN LENT
LECTIONARY READINGS:
Deuteronomy 26:1-11
Psalm 91:1-2, 9-16
Romans 10:8*b*-13
Luke 4:1-13

TEXT: Deuteronomy 26:1-11

PREPARATORY POSTURE: Pick some fruit from a tree or the produce case. Place it in a basket and bring it to the altar. Reflect on the first fruits you have to share.

EXPERIENCE: On the previous Sunday, encourage chil-dren to bring "first fruits" with them to church today. Many children will not be familiar with the harvest motif, so let *first fruits* be fruit brought to the church on the first Sunday in Lent. Gather all the fruit into a basket or baskets, then let the children carry the baskets and lay them in front of the altar. Tell them the story of Moses' coming out of Egypt or the history of their church as you gather around the altar. Have all the children bow down and lift a prayer of celebration for their first Sunday fruits. Be sure to tell the children how the fruit will be used!

SENSES: *Hearing, sight, and touch*

SECOND SUNDAY IN LENT
LECTIONARY READINGS:
Genesis 15:1-12, 17-18
Psalm 27
Philippians 3:17–4:1
Luke 13:31-35

TEXT: Luke 13:31-35

PREPARATORY POSTURE: Visit a hen house. Collect some eggs.

EXPERIENCE: In the Lukan text Jesus speaks of the dangerous mission that he has little time to accomplish. Begin by finding a hidden audio- or videocassette that can be played for the children giving them instructions for a seemingly impossible mission. Gather them close, like a hen gathers her chicks, so they can listen closely.

If you have a particular project in mind, you could lay out some specific instructions, but a general mission to share God's love with others in your community would be sufficient to get children and adults thinking. Talk about what they will need in order to accomplish their mission— help from others, help from God, and so on. If possible, give each child a copy of the cassette to take home. Encourage them to listen to or watch it over and over again, for God's instructions don't self-destruct, but stay with us.

Invite children and adults to a meeting in the next two weeks to discuss ways to embark on a new mission in the name of Christ. Form several teams to accomplish the ideas God will generate among you. Be sure that children are involved and have a voice. They may challenge everyone to a mission no one thought possible!

SENSES: *Hearing, sight, and touch*

THIRD SUNDAY IN LENT
LECTIONARY READINGS:
Isaiah 55:1-9
Psalm 63:1-8
1 Corinthians 10:1-13
Luke 13:1-9

TEXTS: Isaiah 55:1-9; Luke 13:1-9

PREPARATORY POSTURE: Fertilize a plant that has not been productive. Feed someone who is hungry.

EXPERIENCE: Some children know all about fig trees, but the closest most children have come to figs is Fig Newtons. You might want to pass out Fig Newtons and water as a response to the Old Testament text, Isaiah 55:1-9, which offers free food and drink to persons without money. The parable of the fig tree is troublesome, even for adults. Retell the story, but let the children play the part of the fig tree. Plant each one, and then come back each year looking for food. On the third trip, ask the congregation what to do: "Should I cut them down?" The hope is that the congregation will respond in the negative. Pretend to dig around each tree and spread fertilizer. Let another year transpire and encourage them to bloom and grow. An actual fig placed in their hands would be perfect.

Ask the children to relate a time when they were given a second chance. Then give the children plants or seeds and encourage them to make good use of the soil around their homes.

SENSES: *Hearing, sight, smell, taste, and touch*

FOURTH SUNDAY IN LENT
LECTIONARY READINGS:
Joshua 5:9-12
Psalm 32
2 Corinthians 5:16-21
Luke 15:1-3, 11b-32

TEXT: 2 Corinthians 5:16-21

PREPARATORY POSTURE: Spend a day looking at the world through actual rose-tinted glasses. Visit an embassy.

EXPERIENCE: "From now on, therefore, we regard no one from a human point of view." Get a pair of rose-tinted glasses and let the children look at things and people through them. Talk about how God sees us differently through the blood of Christ. A pastor tells the story of a little girl who said God sees us with upside-down eyes. Help some of the children stand on their heads (not those wearing skirts or dresses this morning) so they, too, might see things with upside-down eyes. Upside-down eyes see the first last and the last first. They also see death as the beginning of life.

Appoint the children as ambassadors for Christ. Give

them a list of duties that an ambassador might have. A letter from an actual ambassador might further emphasize the role of one acting on another's behalf.

SENSES: *Touch, hearing, and sight*

FIFTH SUNDAY IN LENT
LECTIONARY READINGS:
Isaiah 43:16-21
Psalm 126
Philippians 3:4*b*-14
John 12:1-8

TEXTS: Philippians 3:4*b*-14; John 12:1-8

PREPARATORY POSTURE: Draw a treasure map complete with clues. Give a child the map and help lead the child to the treasure. Work a crossword puzzle.

EXPERIENCE: Lead the children on a treasure hunt, complete with a treasure map that you found in your Bible. Have them follow the clues, as they would do with the television show or the computer program *Where in the World Is Carmen Sandiego?* Don't hesitate to let adults in the congregation share in solving some of the puzzles. Encourage them as they press on toward their goal. Let the treasure be a picture or symbol of Christ, the Bible, or a copy of "Jesus Loves Me, This I Know" for them to sing together.

In addition to regular clues, you might leave a trail of perfume to follow as you retell the story of Mary's anointing Jesus' feet.

SENSES: *Touch, hearing, smell, and sight*

PASSION/PALM SUNDAY
LECTIONARY READINGS:
Isaiah 50:4-9*a*
Psalm 31:9-16
Philippians 2:5-11
Luke 22:14–23:56 or Luke 19:28-40

TEXT: Philippians 2:5-11

PREPARATORY POSTURE: Touch your head, then your shoulders, your knees, and your toes.

EXPERIENCE: Teach the children the song "Head and Shoulders, Knees and Toes." Emphasize each piece of the song with the following thoughts for the children. Incorporate these images from the Passion into the motions:

Head—Holds the crown of thorns
Shoulders—Carry the cross
Knees—Bent in prayer
Toes—Praise God by reaching out to God on our tiptoes, waving our palm fronds
Eyes—Look to Jesus on the cross as the criminals, the women, or the centurion did
Ears—Listen for Jesus' words from the cross
Mouth—Confesses Jesus Christ is Lord
Nose—Smells the perfume from last Sunday's Gospel lesson, the spices and ointments taken to the tomb, or the vinegar or sour wine from Matthew's Passion text

Whisper to a few children that they are to untie someone's shoes and bring the shoes back to the front. Wait for them to do so. The victims are likely to respond, "Why are you untying my shoes?" Let the children respond, "The

Lord needs them." Talk about the courage of the disciples who were willing to untie a colt that wasn't theirs. Be prepared to respond to the question, "Why wasn't it stealing?" Be sure to give back the shoes before the end of the service.

SENSES: *Touch, hearing, and sight*

EASTER DAY
LECTIONARY READINGS:
Acts 10:34-43
Psalm 118:1-2, 14-24
1 Corinthians 15:19-26
Luke 24:1-12 or John 20:1-18

TEXT: John 20:1-18

PREPARATORY POSTURE: Practice leading the Hokey Pokey.

EXPERIENCE: Dean Bowers was serving the Lula United Methodist Church when I heard him preach on the Hokey Pokey church. For him, it was a useful metaphor; for me, it has become an ancient Easter liturgical dance. You never have to say it is the Hokey Pokey. Merely ask the children to join you in a dance.

Draw an imaginary circle in front of you with your foot. This circle could represent the empty tomb and signify the hesitance of Mary Magdalene to enter the tomb. So as if dipping into a cool pool of water, you enter slowly by putting your right foot into the circle and taking your right foot out. Then place your right foot in again and shake it. Continue by using the left foot, the right hand, the left hand, and finally the whole self.

Easter calls us to put our whole selves in. God in Jesus

49

puts God's whole self into the world, and the world is shaken all about by God's loving self-sacrifice. Realizing the truth of the Resurrection then shakes us all about.

SENSES: *Touch, hearing, and sight*

SECOND SUNDAY OF EASTER
LECTIONARY READINGS:
Acts 5:27-32
Psalm 150
Revelation 1:4-8
John 20:19-31

TEXT: Acts 5:27-32

PREPARATORY POSTURE: Practice the Disappearing Act with a group of children.

EXPERIENCE: Children understand the concept of obedience, although they (and we) may not always practice it. Rather than tell children, "Obey God rather than your mom or dad," use this text as a piece of an exciting story about the apostles, beginning in Acts 5:17, which can be retold with the children's help.

Children love magic tricks, and an early favorite is the Disappearing Act. One child holds up a towel or a bedsheet, and another child hides behind it. The people in the congregation are told to close their eyes while the hidden child slips away. When the cloth is removed, the child has vanished, as the apostles vanished from prison. Depending on the ages of the children, you can make this trick as sophisticated as you like, with the children slipping away during a distraction or when the congregation collectively closes its eyes. The children who slip away should then be found in the pulpit, much to everyone's surprise.

SENSES: *Touch, hearing, and sight*

THIRD SUNDAY OF EASTER
LECTIONARY READINGS:
Acts 9:1-6 (7-20)
Psalm 30
Revelation 5:11-14
John 21:1-19

TEXT: Acts 9:1-6 (7-20)

PREPARATORY POSTURE: Play a game of Red Rover with a group of children.

EXPERIENCE: Play a game of Red Rover where one child is designated as Saul and the others call him to come over to God's side. Send Saul out of earshot and tell the children to let him break through easily the first time. Recall how Saul tried to break up the followers of the Way. Before you call Saul again, flash a bright light in his face, blindfold him, and ask, "Saul, Saul, why do you persecute me?" Have the children call the blinded Saul again and then lead him by the hand over to God's side and make him part of the line. Finish by chanting, "Red Rover, Red Rover, we're glad Paul has come over."

SENSES: *Hearing, sight, and touch*

FOURTH SUNDAY OF EASTER

LECTIONARY READINGS:

Acts 9:36-43

Psalm 23

Revelation 7:9-17

John 10:22-30

TEXT: Psalm 23

PREPARATORY POSTURE: Set the table for meals this week.

EXPERIENCE: As you walk through the Twenty-third Psalm with the children, they will hear the phrase "You prepare a table . . . ." Children are familiar with setting a table because this is a household chore for many of them. If you celebrate the Eucharist, you may want the children to help you set the Communion table. This would be a good day to explain the significance of the items placed on the altar, from paraments to candles to offering plates, as the children help you set the altar for that day. You might ask the children to discuss people they consider to be their enemies and how God can get them through their troubles.

SENSES: *Touch, hearing, and sight*

FIFTH SUNDAY OF EASTER

LECTIONARY READINGS:

Acts 11:1-18

Psalm 148

Revelation 21:1-6

John 13:31-35

TEXT: Acts 11:1-18

PREPARATORY POSTURE: Pray for the vision to deal with any criticism you are facing. Eat a meal of food that you have always been uncomfortable eating.

EXPERIENCE: Re-create Peter's vision using either a bed-sheet with animals painted on or ironed from transfers, or a piece of fabric with animals already printed on it. A fabric store staff can easily suggest alternatives.

The cloth can be lowered over the children using four tall adults or a simple pulley system if your setting allows. Include four-footed animals, birds, and reptiles if possible. Tell the children about the dietary laws dictating that the Jews were not supposed to eat certain animals. Recall the words Peter heard. Walk through this three times. Tell the children what Peter's dream made him do.

Children can tell you who are the insiders and the outsiders in their groups. Peter learned that there were to be no outsiders, but only insiders as Christ united *us* all. We are not to get in God's way by thinking that some people are outside God's love in Christ.

SENSES: *Touch, hearing, and sight*

SIXTH SUNDAY OF EASTER
LECTIONARY READINGS:
Acts 16:9-15
Psalm 67
Revelation 21:10, 22–22:5
John 14:23-29

TEXT: John 14:23-29

PREPARATORY POSTURE: Gather together twelve kinds of fruits. Feast on God's goodness and meditate on John 14:23-29 as you eat one or two pieces of fruit each day.

EXPERIENCE:
Idea #1: Tell the story of King Midas, how everything he touched turned into gold and what a mess that finally got him into. Then tell of King Jesus and how everyone he touches turns to God. Have someone touch each child and turn him or her to face the cross in your sanctuary.

Idea #2: How can we keep Jesus' words today? We can record them on an audiocassette. Ask each child to repeat part of today's text or another verse. Record their voices and give them the tapes of their voices so they might keep Jesus' words with them.

SENSES: *Hearing, sight, and touch*

ASCENSION OF THE LORD/SEVENTH SUNDAY OF EASTER
LECTIONARY READINGS:
Acts 1:1-11/Acts 16:16-34
Psalm 47/Psalm 97
Ephesians 1:15-23/Revelation 22:12-14, 16-17, 20-21
Luke 24:44-53/John 17:20-26

TEXT: Revelation 22:12-14, 16-17, 20-21

PREPARATORY POSTURE: Drink an ice-cold glass of water.

EXPERIENCE:
Idea #1: Help the children locate hidden things in the

church by playing "You're getting warmer." Limit the instructions to hot, cold, and lukewarm. When the child is far away from the object, tell the child "cold." When the child is almost on top of the object, say "hot." For all other places, use the almost useless "lukewarm" so that the children will begin to understand the importance of the two extremes. Perhaps you have an Alpha and Omega in your church they can move toward or search for.

Idea #2: The text states, "And let everyone who is thirsty come." Invite the thirsty to come to the children's moments and offer lukewarm drinks. The children may know John 3:16, but do they know Revelation 3:16? "Because you are lukewarm, and neither cold nor hot, I am about to spit you out of my mouth." In rural Georgia, there is nothing worse than a flat, watered-down, lukewarm Coca-Cola unless it's a Pepsi of the same standing. This is the kind of thing people would spew out of their mouths. You can probably think of similar ideas for your setting. Then offer the thirsty ice-cold glasses of refreshing water as they recall the words in verse 17 about the gift of the water of life.

SENSES: *Touch, hearing, sight, and taste*

DAY OF PENTECOST
LECTIONARY READINGS:
Acts 2:1-21
Psalm 104:24-34, 35*b*
Romans 8:14-17
John 14:8-17 (25-27)

TEXTS: Acts 2:1-21; Genesis 11:1-9

PREPARATORY POSTURE: Build a tower of blocks as high as you can.

EXPERIENCE: Using the text from Genesis 11:1-9, provide some blocks for the children to build a tower of blocks as high as they can. The tower will inevitably topple. Help the children to recall the story of the tower of Babel and the people's attempts to build a tower up to God. Let them know this is the opposite of what happened at Pentecost, as the Spirit came down instead of the people trying to go up.

SENSES: *Touch, hearing, and sight*

TRINITY SUNDAY
LECTIONARY READINGS:
Proverbs 8:1-4, 22-31
Psalm 8
Romans 5:1-5
John 16:12-15

TEXT: Romans 5:1-5

PREPARATORY POSTURE: Pour water from a pitcher into a glass until it overflows. Give thanks for the grace in which we stand.

EXPERIENCE: If possible, buy several sponges that have been compressed until almost flat. (Teacher supply stores as well as teaching resource centers for schools often have such sponge sheets.) Regular sponges will also work. Cut one heart shape out of the sponge, or for a small group, cut enough heart shapes for each child to have one. Pour water out of a pitcher labeled *God's Love* onto a sponge, and watch it expand. Then let the children take the wet sponge and press it onto a dark piece of construction paper as an expression that God's love has been poured into our hearts.

Encourage the children to expand their heart-shaped sponges at home.

SENSES: *Hearing, touch, and sight*

PROPER 4

SUNDAY BETWEEN MAY 29 AND JUNE 4 INCLUSIVE
LECTIONARY READINGS:
(If After Trinity Sunday)
1 Kings 18:20-21 (22-29), 30-39/1 Kings 8:22-23, 41-43
Psalm 96/Psalm 96:1-9
Galatians 1:1-12
Luke 7:1-10

TEXT: Psalm 96

PREPARATORY POSTURE: Learn a new song. Try to write a new song.

EXPERIENCE: The psalmist speaks of singing a new song so this would be a perfect time to teach the children a new song or to help them create a song of their own. If you choose to teach them a new song, use a song that is physically engaging complete with motions. Let the children help teach this new song to the entire congregation.

Creating a new song offers several possibilities as the text refers to the rejoicing earth, the glad heavens, the singing trees, the exalting fields, and the roaring seas. Split the children into five groups, each representing a different piece of creation. Help them come up with noises and motions that can be combined for their own new song. Have props ready for each group such as tree branches for the trees and sea shells for the seas. With a large group, the creative process might take place in Sunday school classes where they would have more time to develop their noises, motions, and even costumes. Be sure to provide ways for children who may not have attended Sunday school to still participate. Share this new song with the congregation.

SENSES: *Hearing, sight, and touch*

PROPER 5

SUNDAY BETWEEN JUNE 5 AND JUNE 11 INCLUSIVE
LECTIONARY READINGS:
(If After Trinity Sunday)
1 Kings 17:8-16 (17-24)/1 Kings 17:17-24
Psalm 146/Psalm 30
Galatians 1:11-24
Luke 7:11-17

TEXT: Galatians 1:11-24

PREPARATORY POSTURE: Look into a bright light.

EXPERIENCE: In his letter to the Galatians, Paul writes about his own conversion experience. Collect letters from members of the congregation who are willing to share with the children about the changes God has made in their lives. Be sure that the language of the letters is such that children will not be excluded by the vocabulary used. Include testimony from those who had dramatic conversions and from others who have grown steadily in the faith. The letters could be read by their authors to the children who can then ask questions or the children could be asked to guess who wrote the letters. After this time of sharing, retell Ananias's story of seeing a vision and going to the street called Straight to lay his hands on Saul. Children will love the part about the scales falling from Saul's eyes. You might even have some fish scales for them to see, touch, and smell. Ask the children if they can think of anyone whom they would not want to lay hands on. Assure them that God will give them strength to touch those who they think are untouchable. Allow them to lay hands on one of those who have shared their testimony in order to encourage that person to share the gospel with others.

SENSES: *Hearing, sight, smell, and touch*

PROPER 6

SUNDAY BETWEEN JUNE 12 AND JUNE 18 INCLUSIVE
LECTIONARY READINGS:
(If After Trinity Sunday)
1 Kings 21:1-10 (11-14), 15-21*a*
Psalm 5:1-8
Galatians 2:15-21
Luke 7:36–8:3

TEXTS: Luke 7:36–8:3; Galatians 2:15-21

PREPARATORY POSTURE: Attend or hold a foot-washing service with the leaders of your church.

EXPERIENCE: Focus on either the woman's actions or Jesus' parable. Set the scene at the Pharisees' table by indicating the posture of those who would be sitting at the table in such a way that their feet were accessible. Hosts often washed the feet of their guests, but this host fails to offer this sort of hospitality. The least risky option would be to dab a bit of perfume on the feet or ankles of each child. The children would probably be more greatly influenced by an act of humility embarked upon by several leaders in the church. Invite these adults to come to the chancel area and wash the feet of the children using a sweet-smelling soap, then drying their feet with a towel. Talk with the children about the great love that has been shown to them by this act of giving. Another option that would address the parable is to use the children to play the debtors, and discuss the feelings of being forgiven of their debts.

On this Sunday or on Father's Day, ask the children how many of them want to follow in their fathers' footsteps. Have footprints traced from an adult's shoes ready to be taped down in spots where a father steps. Be sure he takes extra-long strides. Let the children try to follow in the footsteps, which should be too far away for them to step on without jumping or taking extra steps. The footsteps of our parents and of Jesus go before us and show us the way, but we must take our own steps and leave our own footprints as Christ continues to live and walk in us.

SENSES: *Hearing, sight, smell, and touch*

PROPER 7

SUNDAY BETWEEN JUNE 19 AND JUNE 25 INCLUSIVE
LECTIONARY READINGS:
(If After Trinity Sunday)
1 Kings 19:1-4 (5-7), 8-15*a*
Psalms 42 and 43
Galatians 3:23-29

Luke 8:26-39

TEXT: Galatians 3:23-29

PREPARATORY POSTURE: Add one thing to your out-
fit each day that will remind you that you are being clothed
with Christ.

EXPERIENCE: This week is exactly six months before
Christmas. Children know what it means to be clothed like
Santa Claus, but what does it mean to be clothed with
Christ? To be clothed with Christ means not letting differences divide us, neither slave nor free, Jew nor Greek, male
nor female. It doesn't mean that the differences go away
like having all our Christmas presents wrapped the exact
same way; it means that with Christ inside us the differences don't keep us apart.

For small churches: Have packages (one for each child)
wrapped in many different ways, but with the same gift
inside each one. One at a time, let the children pick which
gift they want, and ask them to tell why. Then have them
all open their gifts at the same time and discuss how it felt
to each receive the same gift.

For large churches: Instead of giving gifts, encourage the
children to bring to church next Sunday a specific item that
addresses a mission need, such as shampoo, wrapped in its
own special way. Then acknowledge that the giving that is
inside is the same, although the gifts on the outside look
different.

SENSES: *Hearing, sight, and touch*

PROPER 8

SUNDAY BETWEEN JUNE 26 AND JULY 2
INCLUSIVE
LECTIONARY READINGS:
2 Kings 2:1-2, 6-14
Psalm 77:1-2, 11-20
Galatians 5:1, 13-25
Luke 9:51-62

TEXT: Galatians 5:1, 13-25

PREPARATORY POSTURE: Visit your neighbors. Get to know their pets.

EXPERIENCE: When I was a kid, I had a dog that could never be taken outside without a leash. If she escaped leash-less, she ran away as quickly as she could. One day, she was hit by a car during an adventure into her newfound "freedom." What she thought was freedom resulted in death. Children often encounter death through their pets, and this may be an opportunity for healing and discussion. Talk about where pets live. Birds live in cages, fish live in tanks, dogs live in houses, cats live wherever they want to, and so on. Why? To keep them safe. Encourage the children to think about dogs and recall Paul's words about biting one another. Paul tells us to live by the Spirit and be guided by the Spirit. The Spirit gives us the freedom we need while maintaining the role of guide. How much freedom should a dog have? A leash protects the dog rather than merely restraining the dog. God's Spirit guiding us does not imprison us but helps keep us from straying.

An invisible dog leash would be a perfect visual aid this Sunday. Consider bringing your own pet with you this Sunday and having a Blessing of the Animals ceremony in the afternoon.

SENSES: *Hearing, sight, and touch*

PROPER 9

SUNDAY BETWEEN JULY 3 AND JULY 9 INCLUSIVE

LECTIONARY READINGS:

2 Kings 5:1-14
Psalm 30
Galatians 6:(1-6) 7-16
Luke 10:1-11, 16-20

TEXT: Luke 10:1-11, 16-20

PREPARATORY POSTURE: Learn to throw a boomerang.

EXPERIENCE: A versatile tool for any church's children's ministry is *Creative Nylon Hoseplay.* A number of options exist for communicating this text with combinations of waste hosiery. The boomerang of peace that Jesus speaks of is given out and comes back if not accepted. Use a hose rocket with a large tail. Pull the rocket back if no one in the congregation catches it. A ball with an elastic band attached or a lifesaver ring with a rope attached would also work. A hose rocket swung over the heads of the children can help them feel that something has come near to them.

Glenn Q. Bannerman's *Creative Nylon Hoseplay,* a wonderful video that demonstrates crafts made from pantyhose, is appropriate for all ages and groups, and is available from: Celebration Services, Inc., P.O. Box 399, Montreat, NC 28757. To order waste nylon hose from L'Eggs Products, send a letter of request (on your church letterhead) and a check for $10 per box (approximately 300 waste hose in each box) to Sara Lee Hosiery, L'Eggs Products, 1901 N. Irby Street, Florence, SC 29501. Make checks payable to Sara Lee Hosiery. Mark check, "For Waste Hose."

SENSES: *Hearing, sight, and touch*

PROPER 10

SUNDAY BETWEEN JULY 10 AND JULY 16 INCLUSIVE

LECTIONARY READINGS:

Amos 7:7-17
Psalm 82
Colossians 1:1-14
Luke 10:25-37

TEXT: Luke 10:25-37

PREPARATORY POSTURE: Stop and help someone in need this week.

EXPERIENCE: The story of the good Samaritan is told in response to a lawyer's question about eternal life. Retell the story as adults or teenagers act out the scenes. Set up a courtroom and bring to trial the three characters who passed by. Allow the children to question the two who passed by about their motives for not stopping. Be sure to ask the Samaritan why he did stop. Corroborating witnesses such as the innkeeper and the victim could also be called. Prepare a number of questions in advance and write them on cards for older children who can read, but do not limit the children to these questions. Provide large name tags for the characters. Discuss the legitimacy of the reasons given with the children.

SENSES: *Hearing, touch, and sight*

PROPER 11

SUNDAY BETWEEN JULY 17 AND JULY 23 INCLUSIVE

LECTIONARY READINGS:
Amos 8:1-12
Psalm 52 or Psalm 15
Colossians 1:15-28
Luke 10:38-42

TEXT: Luke 10:38-42

PREPARATORY POSTURE: Focus on someone in your family and spend time with the person. Try to concentrate on your relationship and interaction without being distracted by the phone, television, or household chores.

EXPERIENCE: Been searching for the opportunity to introduce a screen to the worship setting (without offending anyone and everyone)? Allow children to play the deconstructionist role as you place the screen at the front of the sanctuary for the children's sermon. Project out-of-focus images from slides or an overhead projector onto the screen. Try moving closer and then farther away to see if things can be put back into focus by your movements. Martha's movements don't put things back into focus. Only by concentrating, like Mary, on the One in whose image we are made will things come back into focus. Retell the story of Mary and Martha, letting the children play the roles. Then help the children put things back in focus on the screen. Children will easily relate to Jesus at this point because they, too, are often faced with Marthas who spend an inordinate amount of time on work instead of spending time with them. Children know what it is to compete for attention with household chores.

Use the screen for the rest of the service to show images from Scripture and words to hymns and praise choruses.

SENSES: *Hearing, touch, and sight*

PROPER 12

SUNDAY BETWEEN JULY 24 AND JULY 30 INCLUSIVE

LECTIONARY READINGS:
Hosea 1:2-10
Psalm 85
Colossians 2:6-15 (16-19)
Luke 11:1-13

TEXT: Luke 11:1-13

PREPARATORY POSTURE: Start the week with a fresh loaf of bread. Eat at least one slice each day as you begin a time of prayer.

EXPERIENCE: The children will know the phrase "Give us each [this] day our daily bread" from the Lord's Prayer. We can keep bread fresh for only a few days. If it is not used, it begins to grow mold. Show the children examples of bread that has been kept too long. Jesus tells us to ask God for bread daily in order to always have fresh bread. In the same way, we ask God daily to keep our spiritual life fresh.

Use the counterpoint in "God Help the Outcasts" from Disney's *The Hunchback of Notre Dame* to teach children how to pray. Esmeralda sings a heartfelt prayer for others, while the so-called parishioners sing these self-centered words:

I ask for glory to shine on my name.

In stark contrast, Esmeralda sings,

Please help my people, the poor and downtrod.

SENSES: *Hearing, sight, and touch*

PROPER 13

SUNDAY BETWEEN JULY 31 AND AUGUST 6 INCLUSIVE

LECTIONARY READINGS:
Hosea 11:1-11
Psalm 107:1-9, 43
Colossians 3:1-11
Luke 12:13-21

TEXT: Luke 12:13-21

PREPARATORY POSTURE: Examine your abundance of possessions. Hold a yard, garage, or barn sale.

EXPERIENCE: Talk to the children about what it meant to be the firstborn male child in Jesus' time. Give something all the children would enjoy, such as a bag of candy, to the oldest male child in attendance. Allow him to decide what he wants to do with it: keep it all, share it, or give some of it away. You might also invite all the children to do something fun that takes both hands to do while the oldest male child has his hands full.

SENSES: *Hearing, touch, taste, and sight*

PROPER 14

SUNDAY BETWEEN AUGUST 7 AND AUGUST 13 INCLUSIVE

LECTIONARY READINGS:
Isaiah 1:1, 10-20
Psalm 50:1-8, 22-23
Hebrews 11:1-3, 8-16
Luke 12:32-40

TEXT: Hebrews 11:1-3, 8-16

PREPARATORY POSTURE: Attempt to count the number of grains in a teaspoon of sand.

EXPERIENCE: Play the game The First Step Is Always the Hardest. Lead the children in a game of Mother May I. The leader stands on one side and instructs the children to take certain kinds of steps (baby steps, bunny hops, giant steps, and so forth). The children ask, "Mother may I?" and the leader responds, "Yes, you may," or "No, you may not." Tell the children to take weird steps that they have never heard of. Use the names from the Isaiah text. Take three Uzziah steps or two Ahaz steps. The children will not know where to start. The first step will be difficult because these new steps are unknown. Show the children how to take the first step. After they try the first one, the rest will come easily.

SENSES: *Hearing, sight, and touch*

PROPER 15

SUNDAY BETWEEN AUGUST 14 AND AUGUST 20 INCLUSIVE

LECTIONARY READINGS:
Isaiah 5:1-7
Psalm 80:1-2, 8-19
Hebrews 11:29–12:2
Luke 12:49-56

TEXT: Hebrews 11:29–12:2

PREPARATORY POSTURE: March around something with which you have been struggling.

EXPERIENCE: Children are examples of those who are not predictable or controllable, so the Luke text will be difficult for them to understand. Instead, allow the children to fight the Battle of Jericho alluded to in the Hebrews text. March around the "city," represented by a tower of blocks. Walk around the city once for six "days" with seven children bearing seven trumpets. Kazoos will do. On the seventh "day," march around the city seven times while blowing the trumpets. Then encourage all the children to shout. Have a wall or the stack of blocks tumble over. The walls of Jericho fell not by might, but by faith, believing God's word. See Joshua 6 for additional details.

SENSES: *Hearing, touch, and sight*

PROPER 16

SUNDAY BETWEEN AUGUST 21 AND AUGUST 27 INCLUSIVE
LECTIONARY READINGS:
Jeremiah 1:4-10
Psalm 71:1-6
Hebrews 12:18-29
Luke 13:10-17

TEXT: Hebrews 12:18-29

PREPARATORY POSTURE: Make your own butter.

EXPERIENCE: When all is shaken, what remains? Proverbs 30:33 tells of the churning of milk into butter. Ask the children, "Where do we get butter?" Explain that people have to make butter and that it is what remains after cream has been shaken. Take a small glass jar and fill it with heavy cream, a pinch of sugar, and a pinch of salt. Pass the jar around and let the children shake it as hard as they can. Keep shaking it for about a minute until it turns to butter. Drain off the liquid, buttermilk, that remains and allow the children to taste the butter on bread or crackers during or after church. When all is shaken, only the best remains.

SENSES: *Hearing, sight, smell, taste, and touch*

PROPER 17
SUNDAY BETWEEN AUGUST 28 AND SEPTEMBER 3 INCLUSIVE
LECTIONARY READINGS:
Jeremiah 2:4-13
Psalm 81:1, 10-16
Hebrews 13:1-8, 15-16
Luke 14:1, 7-14

TEXTS: Luke 14:1, 7-14; Psalm 81:1, 10-16

PREPARATORY POSTURE: Give someone an anonymous gift.

EXPERIENCE: My grandfather always told me, "If you

take care of me when I'm old, I'll take care of you when you're old." I knew he could never return the favor, but I helped him as best I could. Children can most easily understand Luke 14:12-14. For children, babies or animals are those who cannot pay them back. Give the children ideas of what they can do for others without expecting to be repaid.

Move to the psalter in order for the children to give something to the congregation for which they will not be repaid, the gift of a song. The psalmist tells us in Psalm 81:1 to "sing aloud to God our strength; shout for joy to the God of Jacob." Teach the children a song of joy such as "The Joy of the Lord Is My Strength," which merely repeats those words four times. Additional verses can be added: "If you want joy, you must [action word] for it." Do the action word such as *clap* to the time set forth in the song for three lines, finishing with "the joy of the Lord is my strength."

Finally, ask the children to open their mouths as wide as they can, assuring them that God will fill them as promised in verse 10. Fill their wide open mouths with honey wheat bread as alluded to in verse 16.

SENSES: *Hearing, touch, sight, smell, and taste*

PROPER 18
SUNDAY BETWEEN SEPTEMBER 4 AND
SEPTEMBER 10 INCLUSIVE
LECTIONARY READINGS:
Jeremiah 18:1-11
Psalm 139:1-6, 13-18
Philemon 1-21
Luke 14:25-33

TEXT: Philemon 1-21

PREPARATORY POSTURE: Take a letter of forgiveness to someone you need to forgive or to someone from whom you need to ask forgiveness.

EXPERIENCE: Philemon is literally a letter asking for forgiveness, the forgiveness of a debt. Prepare a piece of paper for each child on which a large letter is printed. Use the letters F-O-R-G-I-V-E-N-E-S-S. Use FORGIVE with a small group. Lead the children in a forgiveness cheer. Have then hold up their letters when the letters are called out. Gimme an F! Gimme an O! And so on. What's that spell? FORGIVENESS. Ask the children to take their letter to someone from whom they want forgiveness or someone they need to forgive.

SENSES: *Hearing, sight, and touch*

PROPER 19

SUNDAY BETWEEN SEPTEMBER 11 AND SEPTEMBER 17 INCLUSIVE

LECTIONARY READINGS:
Jeremiah 4:11-12, 22-28
Psalm 14
1 Timothy 1:12-17
Luke 15:1-10

TEXT: Luke 15:1-10

PREPARATORY POSTURE: Sweep the floor.

EXPERIENCE: To illustrate the story of the lost coin, one Georgia pastor hides a coin in a hymnal in the sanctuary on this Sunday and allows the children to search until they find this lost coin. You may want to hide several coins or limit the sphere of seeking to the choir loft or chancel.

For the lost sheep, invite all the children to act like sheep and to hide somewhere around the sanctuary while you play Shepherd and Go Seek. Deliberately find all of the children save one. Then try to close with a prayer or go on with the rest of the service. Undoubtedly, the children will not allow you to continue until every sheep is found. Let them finish the search with you, for it seems they already understand the story.

SENSES: *Hearing, sight, and touch*

PROPER 20

SUNDAY BETWEEN SEPTEMBER 18 AND SEPTEMBER 24 INCLUSIVE

LECTIONARY READINGS:
Jeremiah 8:18–9:1
Psalm 79:1-9 or Psalm 113
1 Timothy 2:1-7
Luke 16:1-13

TEXTS: Jeremiah 8:18–9:1; 1 Timothy 2:1-7

PREPARATORY POSTURE: Peel some onions. As you peel back the layers, ponder the layers that have built up in your life. Have a good cry.

EXPERIENCE: Children are quite used to seeing their peers and younger children cry, but seeing adults cry always seems to stop them in their tracks. Even our two-year-old seems to gaze in wonderment when he sees his mother or me cry. Prepare a washcloth saturated with water in a bowl. Wring it out for the children and tell them about Jeremiah's tears, or cut an onion as you talk and let your own tears flow. Jeremiah felt like crying day and night because the people wouldn't listen to God. He asked, "Isn't there any medicine that can help? Isn't there a doctor who can make them better?" Children may have asked the same questions in the midst of pain, sickness, and even death in their families. Allow children to talk about times they have cried, letting them know tears are okay. Even Jesus cried.

Help the children make a list of people for whom they should and want to pray. Include people they think are sad and hurting like Jeremiah. Make the list as long as you can, because we are instructed to pray for everyone. Pray with the children not just for ourselves but for everyone.

SENSES: *Hearing, sight, smell, and touch*

PROPER 21

SUNDAY BETWEEN SEPTEMBER 25 AND OCTOBER 1 INCLUSIVE
LECTIONARY READINGS:
Jeremiah 32:1-3*a*, 6-15
Psalm 91:1-6, 14-16
1 Timothy 6:6-19
Luke 16:19-31

TEXT: Luke 16:19-31

PREPARATORY POSTURE: Walk through a gate. Visit an area where homeless people are likely to gather.

EXPERIENCE: Children will love to hear this story about

a man who has dogs licking his sores. Yet retelling this whole story could be very confusing for children. The key issue is whether or not achieving wealth and success means you have God's favor. Show the children pictures of people who look rich and others who look poor. Ask the children to identify which ones God likes better. Discuss the children's answers, concluding that God loves us all equally. Perhaps the rich man was left tormented not because of his wealth, but because of his lack of compassion for the poor man who sat at the gate. Ask the children, "Have you ever passed by someone in need?"

For World Communion Sunday: One of childhood's greatest concerns is line etiquette. Lines even have a special lingo associated with them. Taking the wrong place in line is a major violation, described as jumping, breaking, and butting, to name a few. Ask the children about the kinds of lines in which they stand and wait. Invite them to stand in God's eternal line as they come forward for Communion. How would they feel if someone broke in front of them to get Communion? Recall Timothy's words calling us to generosity and a willingness to share.

SENSES: *Hearing, sight, taste, and touch*

PROPER 22

SUNDAY BETWEEN OCTOBER 2 AND OCTOBER 8 INCLUSIVE
LECTIONARY READINGS:
Lamentations 1:1-6
Psalm 137
2 Timothy 1:1-14
Luke 17:5-10

TEXT: 2 Timothy 1:1-14

PREPARATORY POSTURE: Write a letter of encouragement to someone.

EXPERIENCE: Call or write someone whom the children admire, such as an ecclesiastical official, a politician, a teacher, a sports figure, a leader in the community or the church, or an entertainer. Ask this person to write a letter of encouragement to the beloved children of your church just as Paul wrote to Timothy. Make enough copies so each child can take these words of encouragement home. You'll be surprised by who will be willing to write back and share his or her faith with a group of children. Include a return address or even an addressed envelope so the children can respond to these words of hope.

SENSES: *Hearing, sight, and touch*

PROPER 23

SUNDAY BETWEEN OCTOBER 9 AND OCTOBER 15 INCLUSIVE
LECTIONARY READINGS:
Jeremiah 29:1, 4-7
Psalm 66:1-12
2 Timothy 2:8-15
Luke 17:11-19

TEXT: Luke 17:11-19

PREPARATORY POSTURE: Wear a Band-Aid on your finger to remind you of God's healing power.

EXPERIENCE: Give a Band-Aid or adhesive bandage to each child. Let the children put the Band-Aids on any scrapes or sores. Do the Band-Aids actually heal the skin? No, the Band-Aids just protect the area that has been hurt. The healing comes from God and the way God created our bodies. Lead the children in a prayer of thanksgiving for the ways we get better when we are sick and the way our wounds heal. One might arrange for a child to come back to say thank you for the Band-Aid after the others have gone back to their seats. Yet the idea is not to make those who didn't say thank you feel guilty, but to have us give thanks to God and praise God for healing that comes through Band-Aids and through other people.

SENSES: *Hearing, sight, and touch*

PROPER 24

SUNDAY BETWEEN OCTOBER 16 AND OCTOBER 22 INCLUSIVE

LECTIONARY READINGS:
Jeremiah 31:27-34
Psalm 119:97-104 or Psalm 121
2 Timothy 3:14–4:5
Luke 18:1-8

TEXT: 2 Timothy 3:14–4:5

PREPARATORY POSTURE: Find a scripture verse starting with each letter of the alphabet, from A to Z.

EXPERIENCE: Begin a children's sermon series this Sunday. With a small group, provide a small notebook or folder for each child. With a large group, maintain one large notebook that the children can have access to during the rest of the week. Add a new page every Sunday. This Sunday's page would have a picture captioned by a word or phrase beginning with A. Next Sunday's word would begin with B, and so on. This series could take the children through half a year (twenty-six weeks). If this is successful, you can continue with numbers. The children will look forward to receiving, creating or coloring each new page and will have something to help them remember their weekly worship experiences. Clip-art images can be enlarged, or a talented artist in the congregation might take on this project. The phrase for this Sunday could be verse 16*a*: "All scripture is inspired by God." This could be placed under a picture of the Bible.

SENSES: *Hearing, sight, and touch*

PROPER 25

SUNDAY BETWEEN OCTOBER 23 AND OCTOBER 29 INCLUSIVE
LECTIONARY READINGS:
Joel 2:23-32
Psalm 65
2 Timothy 4:6-8, 16-18
Luke 18:9-14

TEXT: Luke 18:9-14

PREPARATORY POSTURE: Come into the church to pray. Examine your prayer posture.

EXPERIENCE: Enlist two youths or adults to play the parts of the Pharisee and the tax collector. Tell the children good things about Pharisees, including the way Pharisees were seen by others in those days. Encourage them to yell "Yea!" every time the Pharisee is mentioned. Then tell them less-than-desirable things about tax collectors and the perception of tax collectors in Jesus' day and in ours. Have them yell "Boo!" every time tax collectors are mentioned.

After the stage has been set, ask the children to be quiet and watch what happened when these two came to the Temple to pray. Direct the actors to overplay their parts as they retell the story. "Which of these two went home justified, right with God?" Let the children decide who and why. It is hoped they will see a new side to the tax collector. ("Yea!") What happens when we think we are better or more important than other people? Talk with the children about their own prayers.

SENSES: *Hearing, sight, and touch*

PROPER 26

SUNDAY BETWEEN OCTOBER 30 AND NOVEMBER 5 INCLUSIVE
LECTIONARY READINGS:
Habakkuk 1:1-4; 2:1-4
Psalm 119:137-44
2 Thessalonians 1:1-4, 11-12
Luke 19:1-10

TEXT: Luke 19:1-10

PREPARATORY POSTURE: Climb a tree. Invite yourself to dinner.

EXPERIENCE: To stress the role of Jesus in this story,

bring the children to the front of the church and have them each look for a person in the congregation who needs to hear good news. Have the children go to the persons they have picked and tell them, "Jesus loves you."

To stress the role of Zacchaeus, invite the youth of the church to come forward first and gather tightly around a large box with a picture of Jesus in the bottom. Then invite the younger children. Make it difficult for the younger children to see what is in the box. Watch for resourceful children and the lengths to which they will go in order to see what is in the box. Invite some of the adults to help the younger children see. The children can then talk about how Zacchaeus must have felt and how good it felt to finally get to Jesus. What would they do if Jesus invited himself over for lunch at their house today?

SENSES: *Hearing, sight, and touch*

PROPER 27

SUNDAY BETWEEN NOVEMBER 6 AND NOVEMBER 12 INCLUSIVE
LECTIONARY READINGS:
Haggai 1:15*b*–2:9 or Job 19:23-27*a*
Psalm 145:1-5, 17-21 or Psalm 17:1-9
2 Thessalonians 2:1-5, 13-17
Luke 20:27-38

TEXT: 2 Thessalonians 2:1-5, 13-17

PREPARATORY POSTURE: Do twenty minutes of aerobic exercise each day to strengthen your heart.

EXPERIENCE: Find something difficult to stand on, such

as a partially inflated/deflated ball. Balance boards may be readily available at a local school gym. Have the children attempt to stand on whatever item you chose. At first, do not help them balance, but be there to catch them when they begin to fall. Help them recognize that without help one cannot stand firm on something unsteady. God helps us stand firm even when we lose our balance.

An exercise illustrating standing firm and holding fast to help the children strengthen their hearts is another option.

SENSES: *Hearing, sight, and touch*

PROPER 28

SUNDAY BETWEEN NOVEMBER 13 AND NOVEMBER 19 INCLUSIVE

LECTIONARY READINGS:
Isaiah 65:17-25 or Malachi 4:1-2*a*
Isaiah 12 or Psalm 98
2 Thessalonians 3:6-13
Luke 21:5-19

TEXTS: Malachi 4:1-2*a* (2*b*-6); Luke 21:5-19

PREPARATORY POSTURE: Drive around your community and identify warning signs such as *Falling Rocks* or *Children at Play.*

EXPERIENCE: Because this Sunday marks the end of the ordinary days between Pentecost and Christ the King, it is appropriate to deal with a text that marks the end of the Old Testament. Ask the children to locate Malachi. Have Bibles available for the older children. When they find Malachi, send them to the last verses of the book. Move through the text with the children, pointing out images like cows leaping in their stalls. Explain that Malachi is telling us there will be a day when God will wipe out evil and all the bad things in the world. Some people want to predict when this will happen, but Jesus in Luke 21 reminds us that no one knows the hour. We are given a warning that it is to happen, but not an exact day, date, or time. Malachi tells us to remember the laws of Moses, which the children will know as the Ten Commandments. Malachi 4:5 speaks of Elijah the prophet being sent back. Indicate that was why so many people compared John the Baptist to Elijah. Prepare the children for John's arrival during Advent. Ask the children about warnings they have received. Warnings help us be more careful and keep us safe. Emphasize that warnings are not meant to scare us, although sometimes they do.

Another idea: Ask the children to react to the verse, "Anyone unwilling to work should not eat." Do they do their fair share of work? What is wrong with being lazy? When we are lazy, we are wasting the good things, the talents God has given us. Everyone gets tired, but we should not get tired of doing good things. Ask the children about the good things they are doing, the good things their Sunday school classes are doing, their families, the church, and so on. Consider giving the children a job to do at the church after the worship service and feeding them lunch or a snack when the task is completed.

SENSES: *Hearing, sight, taste, and touch*

PROPER 29

SUNDAY BETWEEN NOVEMBER 20 AND NOVEMBER 26 INCLUSIVE

(Last Sunday After Pentecost or Christ the King)

LECTIONARY READINGS:

Jeremiah 23:1-6

Luke 1:68-79 or Psalm 46

Colossians 1:11-20

Luke 23:33-43

TEXT: Jeremiah 23:1-6

PREPARATORY POSTURE: Clean out your toolbox. Put away any tools that are not in the proper place around the house.

EXPERIENCE: "What time is it, everybody? It's Tool Time!" Invite the children forward for "Tool Time," as seen on the popular television show *"Home Improvement."* Ask them to identify the different tools we need as Christians. Include the Bible, the cross, and the church. Invite one or two shepherds to come forward for each child. Use parents, relatives, Sunday school teachers, and others who can act as shepherds for these children. Commission the adults as shepherds, reminding them of the tools they will need to care for their sheep, so the sheep will not fear or be dismayed. Include in the commission an admonition to strengthen the homes of these children. Give the shepherds a nail to remind them of Christ's sacrifice for us and their commissioning as homebuilders/shepherds. As seen in the Jeremiah passage, shepherds can be either constructive or destructive. Nails share the same possibilities.

SENSES: *Hearing, sight, and touch*

NOTES

1. Sam Matthews, "Learning Like Children," *Wesleyan Christian Advocate*, 9 September 1994, p. 5.
2. Carolyn C. Brown, *Gateways to Worship* (Nashville: Abingdon Press, 1989), p. 8.
3. William Armstong, *Five Minute Sermons to Children* (New York: The Methodist Book Concern, 1914), p. 6.
4. David Elkind, *The Hurried Child* (Reading, Mass.: Addison-Wesley, 1981), p. 97.
5. Leander Keck, *The Church Confident* (Nashville: Abingdon Press, 1993), p. 104.
6. Dick Murray, *Teaching the Bible to Adults and Youth* (Nashville: Abingdon Press, 1987), p. 57.

SCRIPTURE INDEX – YEAR C _____

Genesis
11:1-9...55

Deuteronomy
26:1-11..43

2 Kings
2:1-12..42

Psalms
23..52
81:1, 10-16 70
96..57

Isaiah
9:2-7...33
55:1-9...45

Jeremiah
1:4-10...38
8:18–9:1 73
23:1-6...83

Micah
5:2-5a...32

Malachi
3:1-4...30
4:1-2a (2b-6)...81

Matthew
2:1-12...35

Luke

2:1-14 (15-20) 33
2:41-52..33
3:7-18..31
3:15-17, 21-22 35
4:14-21 38
5:1-11..39
6:17-26..40
6:27-38..41
7:36–8:3...59
9:28-36 (37-43 42
10:1-11, 16-20 63
10:25-37..64
10:38-42..65
11:1-13..66
12:13-21..67
13:31-35..44
13:1-9..45
14:1, 7-14 70
15:1-10..72
16:19-31..74
17:11-19..76
18:9-14..78
19:1-10..79
21:5-19..81
21:25-36..29

John

2:1-11..37
12:1-8..47
14:23-29..53
20:1-18..49

Acts

2:1-21..55
5:27-32..50
9:1-6 (7-20) 51
11:1-18..53

Romans

5:1-5..56

2 Corinthians

5:16-21 46

Galatians

1:11-24 58

2:15-21 59

3:23-29 61

5:1, 13-25 62

Philippians

2:5-11 48

3:4b-14 47

2 Thessalonians

2:1-5, 13-17 80

1 Timothy

2:1-7 73

2 Timothy

1:1-14 76

3:14–4:5 77

Philemon

1-21 71

Hebrews

11:1-3, 8-16 68

11:29–12:2 69

12:18-29 70

Revelation

22:12-14, 16-17, 20-21 54